Ruins, Ruminations, and Rituals

Poems by Bryon Cherry

Published by Anarcho Welfare Press
anarchowelfare.com

contents

Clank

Synchronizing the world of commerce,
into a synthesis of packages, carbon emissions and American lives made more and
more at a somehow uneasy ease.

The dinosaurs gave their lives for this.

Clank, clank, clank, clanking, the brown truck carries a cacophony of boxes tumbling
and reorganizing themselves as the truck is spurred on with the not quite so
dense traffic's draft.

The driver, the deliverer, the anointed, the proficient at bearing capitalistic provisions,
sits for what is a bumpy ride in old brown truck.

His only destination today is a large office building converted from the old Charles Allis
factory, where during the second great war pieces of the atomic bombs which
devastated, devastated, devastated millions of lives across the world in Japan,
were built, built, built.

76 years, or so, after the building of devastation inducing slaughter machine pieces, it
can be assumed that all of those with a hand in their production are deceased just

like the Japanese who were incinerated before they could blink, their shadows still burned into the ground.

The delivery man, 5′4 but stout with military grade haircut, delivers from one quiet office space to the next. Two packages here and four here and other numbers of packages there.

He then steps back into the 65 degree cool early June morn and wipes his brow.

Then clank, clank, clank the brown truck goes back to the intermittent midday traffic of I-94 now headed eastbound back, back, back to the expansive fulfillment warehouse, where 10 doll
at an hour employees ready, with supervised, mechanically-assisted frenzy, his next junket of deliverance.

A Trip to Target (6.3.17)

I want to view every piece of film that was ever taken of me for security footage.
I want to decide that a garment might be able to merge, in simple closet, with clothing
that is used in a bifurcated manner, that is for cover and ratcheting up a sense of
self.

Backtracking always stimulated the fear and anxiety centers of the three pound,
hundred billion neuron containing architect of my reality; today though, in this
store, with this wife, with this 16 month old son, those moments that were fraught
with irrational trepidation are replaced by something.

I pause to think about this because my wife suggests we backtrack to the infant shoe
section, to procure summer sandals, for his absolution feet, so clean- as if they
were of the disciples' feet in the hands of the master.

We got there, and a pair of blue and neon yellow rubber sandals, with a velcro strap
were put on the laughing 16 month old and they fit.

The wife said, "$23.95".
"$23.95? Hell, he'll only wear them for a month," I quipped.
I did not mean it but it was true.

I do not want to exist merely counting the days between pay periods but I do.

I push the red cart holding our mixed child with an emerging lilt curl to his sandy hair, whose complexion is of a Caucasian with an eternal early July midwestern tan.

The cart's color emulates the palate of the entire store, noticing this I shatter the fourth wall of branding and I wonder how many marketing meetings were held to decide that all this focus on the once parted sea's pigment would make me one day push my son past a green with white swirls plastic ball and feel my son reach out and vocally yearn for it.

In which marketing meeting was it sussed out that the primal need for a father to collect items that might make his child, his family happy, if only for a moment, would manifest itself in this artificially well-lit consumer nature experiment?

I guess that is of little matter now because the green plastic ball is now in my red plastic and metal cart as my brown face smiles in unison with the eternally early July midwestern tanned face of my son.

As we proceed, my wife makes jokes about not needing anything as she gently places everything into the cart.

We backtrack some more and I do not even think about what backtracking used to activate in my brain's amygdala area until I get time to process and reflect upon the capitalistic adventure much later.

We get into checkout line two and after two minutes and 17 seconds of waiting, I wonder out loud if we have selected the wrong line.

My wife laughs it off and we wait, another 3 minutes and 41 seconds then the cashier
does what cashiers do, with our selected items. He also was able to squeeze in
some time for awkward banter and jokes that were laughed at by us in part to be
polite but laughed at in no part because they were funny.

"Your total is $98.68, you saved $26.42 today," he said.

Does that mean we have won?

My wife then inserted chip laced card into chip card reader and invisible monetary
funds were invisibly flooded from her account to the store's provisions.

We then left the chain store, somehow chained and unchained as I pushed the red cart,
as my son held green ball.

The 16 month old then hit the ball and wind, on an almost 80 degree day, took the ball
across the parking lot.

A kind professional cart wrangler with dreadlocks and kind eyes chased it clear across
the parking lot and brought it to me. I thanked him and told him not to work too
hard because that is a stock line of mine that usually returns a knowing smile and
laugh.

We unload our red cart into my silver hatchback. I go to put away our red cart when I
see another red cart that a patron has carelessly let stray in the middle of the
parking lot in front of my silver hatchback.

I collect the strewn, abandoned red cart and push my red cart into it, the way they were
intended to fit together. I push both red carts into the red cart holding area.

I get into my car and drive away with my wife and 16 month old.

Perhaps we are all just washing each other's feet in one way or another, rinsing off life's
grime to reveal the holy in our self and the other.

Meliorism and Golden Facades

Something about how all towns look the same.

Brick facades, veneers thinly layered across McDonald's and pancake houses. Facades
of security, oh the security of facades.

A species with an eternal rut and ample internalized trauma chews its cud slowly and
briefly considers the transactional adventures to come, which are conveniently
located in this same vacuously poignant plaza.

Meliorism, or at least the belief in it, has seemed to carry the day.

That nothing needs to be better is apparently a thought for losers, too caught up in their
losses to join in on the never extinguished story of a sacred destiny made
manifest.

Something about the poem's narrator's desire for change but feeling powerless.

Sex Like This

There is no time for escape, so it takes precedence that one escapes through the
     rough, ragged utilization of an ever-moving, lacking a defined plan, multiverse.
     The electrons they repulse here, what is it that they do when they miraculously
     leave here?

A waning tomb, mid-summer, mid-apocalypse, mid-forever on the mend.
The ever-bent nature of one's mind.
The curtains must be fixed, and I can't have sex like this.

If one is honest, isn't one just a little bit tired?

Tired. An entitled to the whole vast expanse of the nothingness of space struggle.

Ensnared like dying rabbit in a mid-1800's trapper's snare.

Ultimately. Ultimately. Ultimately.

A coin where both sides mirror massive illusion.

Duality, central theme of a world which considers itself modern.

Everyone who has lived, will live or is currently living has or will give their life in pursuit
     of an antidote.

A maybe antiquated notion swirls in our tender, receiving and giving psyches.
Brothel dreams, where one may become his essence's spinning out of control nature,
     like the voracious dead and alive
blackhole, into which all matter, black or not, will migrate, whether it chooses to
     sacrifice itself to the moment or risks its being to run from this convincing
     manifestation.

The Last Evening of May, 2017

The Bootes constellation is reigning over the section of sky where my house rests. We
   have owned the home for exactly ten years and a little over one month. Timeless
   Bootes is hanging in the sky with his staff held high and proud.

Something about the way that J.P. Morgan Chase allows me to feel like I really do own
   this home turns me the fuck on.

So, with my wife I've planted three lilac bushes, two of them purple and one white,
   against my one car garage.
They are my wife's favorite and when, after harsh winter, I get to stand and watch her
   nuzzle up to them and luxuriate in their potent ancient aromas, I am nothing but a
   manifestation of their sweet fragrance.

I grill asada chicken breasts from Trader Joe's along with hearty asparagus stalks which
   are lightly salted and tossed in olive oil. My sixteen month old son stumble walks
   over the uneven freshly cut grass and mutters "buh-bye" to the universe and no
   one in particular.

Jenny, a friend, whose friendship has soared beyond meaning, is on the other end of my
   cellular device. It is the second anniversary of her mother's death. The mournful
   tones emanating from her, while she is five hours away in her Northwoods
   Wisconsin abode, are filled with questions about life's ultimate meaning. The
   offered phrases I send to her seem hollow to me, so I listen more than talk as she
   attempts to unspool the spiderwebs of grief that only seems to ensnare her tired,

wearied mind-heart more and more. We bid each other adieu with open and true pronouncements of love.

The sky above is clear and the degrees of temperature linger around seventy in Fahrenheit measurements. I suggest we eat outside on our humble new patio furniture. The three of us decide that open air eating feels right; we talk about our current forks in life's ever-changing roads and we laugh and sing with the 16 month old who somehow arose from sacred components of us, just as we somehow arose from sacred components of longdead stars.

My Eyes Caught a Glint

Corneas, unsure, gather light refractions from the wet ground for three seconds then meet the other tiny human's light refractors.

Her diminutive arm is reaching, already, towards his nascent male energy.

Swirling around the two of them, there are arms splayed on bars apparently made of monkeys and young bottoms gliding along with the incomprehensible, steady gravity down, down, down the metaphor imbued slide.

The boy, hued with melanin contemplated her question.

He questioned his meaning.

She wondered with mouth arched primal, hungry for an unknown.

He saw her hand as a lilly but as it meandered through the burnt fall, new school year air, it seemed as opaque as a silkworm's tenuous threads.

Turbulence traded places with his usually calm infested mind.

Then in a moment that reflected futures and pasts that had coalesced, he said, "It's alright, you can touch my hair."

The dead follicles of wiry, midnight fuzziness decompressed under the weight of her now knowing hand.

This was the moment where he learned the meaning of the word other, he comprehended it by discovering that he was now, in fact the other.

The spring rabbits are carving out the vocation which they were brought forth for in the
   dandelion strewn backyard.
Caressing sod freshly unburdened of lithe snow.

Tenderly, yet feverishly, paws like cloud-based earth movers plod the no longer
   deadened dirt aside.

This backyard is 30x50 foot plot locked into itself by an unfinished red cedar fencing.

The dwelling attached to the area is adorned in winter-grey siding.
In the morn time when the Sun hits about 80 degrees above the land in its rise, the
   home's windows throw ornate, prismatic reflections onto the similarly grey
   outfitted garage which is semi-covered by white and purple lilacs in early,
   gloriously ambrosial bloom.

It is hard to say if the rabbits notice any of this.

With the focus of a mirror with its penetration to a soul they dig. Every morning they
   dig. Every morning they dig until depth is reached, depth orchestrated by an
   innate knowing and unknowing. This is the sacred negative space where the bulb
   of their species will try to beat the odds and frolic into the future.

Human inhabitant, male, melanin accentuated skin, hair coarse- a kinky morning mess,
   lets his wolf-descended companion out into the yard to defecate and urinate.

Down three concrete stairs the canine bounds, excited by smells, sounds and textile
   touchstones of the outdoors.

It is 5:56 in the am when the domesticated animal's tame restraints break and it sees
   the rabbits laboring in its territory.
Suddenly, the will of predator instincts takes hold and a scene that has played out since
   time immemorial rages in the crucible patch of parcel.

By 5:59 the prey has found the sweet spot to freedom underneath the fence.

The human, takes note of their exit.
In his head he half-awakenly mutters, "I'll have to put a brick there."

Myths

Your locust skin ambles through the stores that are hugging us like prisons. Patiently,
we have crawled out of the dust. We fire our monster's tomahawk missiles at the
other monsters to appease appetites we toil for.

The sky is a gauzy shade of blue and our personal demons scream for the Sun's
madness. You stand alone, aside me. From the effect of your haphazard words, I
seem to glean that this will be alright. A child puts shaking hand to his shadow. A
shadow takes a child in.

Wildly, the bloodbath marches on into oblivion. We have less but spend more of a
human construct, desperately trying to fill a bottomless sinkhole in our soul.

Patriarchy, autonomous nations and too many other myths to keep track of, fight for a
centered place.

Caffeinated mornings and alcohol paced nights. Selling and trading ourselves to binge
on clammy comforts.

My locust skin ambles after you as you make your inescapable exchange at the register.
Should I also buy an impulse Coke for the road? It is after all so conveniently
located right in my purchasing power's periphery.

Perhaps the next crusade will rage against consciousness and its slavery emblazoned
apparition apparatus.

Sklent

In the morass of life and we are in the building aglint with flame.
We are also somehow rushing into the frenzied edifice to somehow save ourselves.

The hallowed horns played sklent lines that sketched the surreal situation.

Never mind all of that, are the car keys really lost?

Do I have time to talk about God?

Why haven't I cut my fingers' nodular nails?

Wefted into a daily practice is the fight for an opportunity to engage in the fight.
We fight for the fortuity to suckle from the honeyed dual teats of humbleness and grace.

Cuddling with loss, and coddling providence, madly waltzing in the darkness tinged light.

Crumbling rain drops now make haste to-heads, shoulders, burning edifices and ground.

That now invisible moment filled with ancient fears is now not even a memory.
Ancestors, unperceivable but persistent, guide ash leadened hands forward; the only
 direction.

Untitled #33

Pace set at incite.
Riot images.
Special coverage.
Bold texted lettering.
Excited noble gases.
Emotional the intellect.
Grasshopper on a newly budding lotus.
Surface conversations.
Suspended are the animations.
The tease of skin grazing skin.
Kin searching out and coalescing with kin.
Mutually assured inception.
Praise hands.
Thin wispy light filaments.
Heart monitors aflame.
The chorus chirps the song.
This fractal nature.
This fractal nature.

A Vision of the Primitive

Your iron eyes;
Resolute yet humbled.
From a stilted, quilted song, sprang an omen.
Rustic, your fair maiden hair.
Lights jam their way on these damp, decorated horizons.
A black/white heifer,
takes gentle knowing head back into full transformative moo.
The Colorado River is hundreds of miles away—
Yet still, I can feel its curves haunting me.
Montezuma, much gold but still died an empty grisly death.
Much death hath happened and even more shall occur.
Occult paradigms become co-opted over time's sacrificial offering to pay heed to that
    death.

Monday Morning Commute

There are seemingly enlightened monkeys hurtling through time and space in 3,100 monkey made pounds of glass, metal and explosive material.

There are monkeys in relationships quarreling until they feel something and perhaps ignite some pyrite lust.

Some of the monkeys have exploited imprinted desires for social orders to place themselves in control.

Another monkey enslaves others cryptically by playing on primordial wants for security and offering ultimately fictitious money in exchange for lives.

Monkeys mundanely masturbating in darkened rooms by themselves because some monkey sexual proclivities seem easier hidden in this monkey made modernity.

Every ingenious idea that the monkeys had, have or will have. Has, is or will be co-opted by a monkey made capitalistic notion and its constant suck of young blood.

Monkeys in tanks, in ships, and on foot, lobbing ballistic warheads, missiles and bullets at each other with eyes closed to nothing but a myth.

Monkey genes, imbued with monkey aggression. Monkey genes tangled in a struggle for more and its inherent toil.

Monkey named concepts like love, hate and also all those in between are in conflict with monkey made theories about what they truly come from.

Monkey fingers to monkey made smartphone keyboard. Monkey brain disseminating monkey hopes, fears and desires about literally being a monkey in time and space driving a car and combating monkey thoughts surrounding trivial monkey life.

Untitled #22

Binary thinking.
Horns aplenty above the devil's mighty mantle.

Tracing insignificant existences around tumbled, troubled trails.
Oh, the dark urge to accumulate.

Acquire, consume and nourish an addled addiction.
Entrails are laid fresh, the wolf hovers his kill, nearby a cobalt stream bludgeons its
      adversarial banks.

The wolf's tongue is to the wind; tasting blood and the silt of generational intent.

Untitled #11

Nucleation points.
She tosses her flaxen hair.
The spiritual sounds of flamenco.
A composed bartender.
A supposition.
A digression.
Then,
A flash bang in a Southern protest.
Police, riot gear.
Stars falling through an hourglass.
Life a constant creation.
Here, serenity. There, chaos.
A lyrical consecration.
It might be over soon.

Untitled #44

Diurnally the citizens commence
About their customs.
The soap is still there,
Where they left it,
So they wash armpits full of yesterdays
Blessings and affronts.
Their teeth get brushed while
Expectations expound
From their weary minds.
They unfold clothing,
Put on clothing and then
Get into cars, trucks, suvs and on to bikes.
Go to places, buildings and structures
Filled with great heights.
In these places they move
With intentions to shake
The foundational underpinnings of infinity.
Infinity though, has its designs
On other laughing lessons.
The citizens encounter other citizens
Who are also searching for meaning.
Everything in its right place so
Interactions bend both bad and good.
Little indignities and small triumphs

Seem to merge during the work day.

After 8 hours or 10 hours or more hours

The citizens bid adieu to the other citizens

And make their way into the natural light.

They get into cars, trucks, suvs and on to bikes- a postscript full of nagging questions.

Diurnally the citizens culminate their duties,

Seemingly to freedom but perhaps only until the next day.

Clearness of Eyes

Aspirations, applications sublimations, animations, ancient Greek salutations, heart palpitations, historical anticipation.

The flood, the drug, the Messiah's handshake. Ruinous remnants of replicating hawks and snakes. Prey and predator intertwined as one.

Landmark, earmark; the lead crow is away, still the murder, murders on. Opening salvation salvo. Whites of their eyes, only then with the gun play.

A test, a testament to the new one. God loves and challenges his kids. Organ solo, the tent revival bursting at the seems with impregnated dreams. A star child's silent shrill scream.

Walk them heels across a heart. Cross your body and eliminate death philosophically but do nothing to keep the fear of it at any bay.

The basis of a system which devours its children for its players gains. Gains still only imaginary, a demonstration of a reckless rhetoric.

Aspirations, clear-eyed reservations, many reasons for hesitations. Drinking and swallowing the vehicle of illumination. A star child's silent shrill scream, soothing and serenading the unconscious but fully cognizant minds.

Dead Heat of Short Summer

Leave me your celestial convictions.
Frolicking manically as Ursa Major prowls on.

It is dead heat Summer in the Northern design.
On the grind down towards the valley,

so that I may appreciate the mountains.
Divinity, flames of a midnight kiln.

Sacred to the sacred;
the moon has its light,

the sun has its fight.
Dormant natures bubble as acid precipitation precipitates.

Through it seems it is this dusty ground, that we must end up.
So clever, the reminiscent revelations.

Mystic tears from Piscis Austrinus.
Something like a dove free-fall.

Dovetailing throughout wild horizons.
Freeform chemical desperations.

Those chemicals are desperate,
desperate to compute their function.

Way too gone for this to be collusion.
Take a picture, of war underneath the cloudless virgin skies.

Surface tension, multiplying dimensions.
Placating, elevating, happy jumping under an indifferent Sun.

Dim Silent Din

Four blinded surging horsemen left my hand and followed the dice as they cascaded along the green table.

The die had been cast.

Maybe our shared dalliance into the normalization of broken behavior was our muddied crossing of the Rubicon.

I lost my ass again on those damn impotent dice.

Collections of reticent cognition then pulled me kicking and screaming to you.

The last vestige of you; you not yelling but horrifically calm.

Eyes deep of hazel and rigidly resolute.

You did not exactly say that you had more than enough of me and my trauma-induced deficiencies.

Still, I conjured the strength to watch you walk away.

The siren-calling flashing lights and the cooing noises of the casino snapped me out of my excursion to my Helen Hell.

Helen, who burst in and had placed her money on me.

Me who placed my money on wild women and guitars.

So, with that I left the sad, robotic nature of the betting den.

I sat firmly in my car, turned up Jason Isbell's "Songs That She Sang in Shower" and
   mutter-cried to myself and no god in particular.

Lush, Slush of Humanity

The lucent nature of sentient beings.
The lush adaptiveness shared amongst them.
The cobbled patchwork linking one to another.

Drawn to the dakini and their beautiful mess.
The hazy restlessness keeping them moving on.
Dutiful, constant striving imprinted on unfortunate bones.

Translucent electrical pulses emanating from gray matter.
Stars erupting from naive, longing eyes.
The feeling of losing to the ultimately insignificant nature of the void.

Joyfully dancing through the weariness and setbacks.
All just projections of a untold number of molecules crashing against the emptiness of
    space.

Untitled #20

Human genetics.
Periscope sightline—
Only pointing at self.
Pointedly missing,
The whole.
Shifting points,
Depictions of the gods.
Dividing line in history.
Notions of a dead ocean.
This is a house of a passion.
New Love,
Sent from above
And down and around
From below.
Can you hear me now?
A shawl draped lazily
Around her ample figurine.
Tangential, self-referential.
Influential mortals who
Are not here.
A collapsing society,
Beckons halfway through
A rich ritual suicide.
The prophet calls upon

Those who sift through
History's dead and buried.
A parable parade of
Polemic, painted parabolas.
Hands on the water.
Estuary savant.
Confluence of consecrated
Meticulous sacraments.
A dreadful sorrow beckons,
We crossed an even line today.
Breaking in horses,
Coalescing forces.
Bones, calcification.
Montezuma's sacked Gold.
Heart in antipathy
To this wrangled joyous horizon.
Sparse Spartan stoicism,
Parading through the
Cracked daylight.

All in All

Swallowed by the ground,
The drunkard inconsolable.

The night sky is engorged,
Engorged with stars counting humans.

Wild women coy,
Outstretched towards the vacant sea.

Leaning into benedictions
From a vagrant homily.

Forms Which Can Occur

Pyramids and The Colosseum.
"Send it over with a little cover memo,
explaining the key parts," exhales the businessman.
Slaughter the swine humanely.
The halcyon eternities of youth.
Clutter collected in a quiet unfinished attic.
Polo shoes, black and gray, on the feet of a middle class American.
Free radicals, unstoppable chain reactions.
Second coat of white paint concealing an ocean teal.
Quite the work ethic.
Heaps of space trash- earth's earned halo.
Adverse childhood events.
Unknowing characters in a play.
Washing dishes before the Sun seeks acclivity.
Celebrity death.
Dustbowl dreams.
Parents fight over text message about having a second child.
Joyful silence amongst friends and lovers.
Self-aware, overreaching, formless poetry.
Stiff winter winds.
Municipalities planting Oak trees.
Left palm itching.
Racing on spinning plates.
Singularity still birthing space.

Taking in an outdoor concert.

Accelerant applied to an addiction.

Cygnus soaring in the summer night sky.

Animalistic, captivating sex wrapped with human guilt.

A golden spear waving savior.

The saturated fat choir, song-less.

A failed state beheaded.

Negative emotionality.

Thousands of nameless African kings.

Meaning courts [aggressively] the illusion.

Phones, Facebook and pervasive fears.

University loans, Sisyphus allusions.

18 month old plays with his stir-fry dinner.

Evolutionary aesthetics embedded and enflamed.

A hailstorm in midwestern America in July.

Magellan's map makers now mostly anonymous.

Meditation under a withering Moon, a Korean young adult lets her thoughts disperse.

Domesticated wildlife.

All of the types of clouds.

A blackout with a humming, working generator.

A three year old calendar, devout and silent.

Image document scanner.

Bombs, jails and innocent children.

Hit repeat on favorite song.

Pagan myths infused into current religions.

Five friends whitewater rafting.

Coffee, marijuana, cocaine, heroin, lithium, abilify, adderall, nicotine, alcohol, ecstasy
and tylenol.
Rats scurrying from trash assemblage to trash assemblage.
Gravity pulling the sled faster, faster down the snow-laden hill.
Cartoons for children and live action dramas for adults.
Patriarchy, psalms and sins.
This dog has a tick.
The man who made up vampires.
Fried chicken with a side of macaroni and cheese.
Databases, freebasing information.
The depraved destruction of Hasanlu.
Baby dolls.
Lotion onto dried out skin.
The anticipation of waiting for a loved one at the airport's baggage claim.
A corn husk thrown away.
The Spanish language.
Fumigating a derelict home.
Distended stomach; the death of another child soon.
Rocking those red heels around mid-town Manhattan.
Casinos padding only a few tribe's coffers.
The ephemeral erection of a delicate ship in a bottle.
Semantics and cinematic climatic circus sprawl.
West coast rap videos in the 1990's.
"I think we're in a good place."
Hypernovas fueling the feasting upon of the blurred galactic time scale.

Blue, Blue Ra

Up this morning and I watch you softly.
You are an emblem of an early riser.

I see the gold, encrusted,
captured around your essence.
Harsh vulnerability.

I hope you remember
the lasting vestiges of your youth.

I can trace them with my rough
and dirty hands. It is not hard for me.

I stand here throwing the moon in the sun's face.
I find it concerning the lives you lead.

And I heave my invisible knives
in an attempt to bring you back.

Blackened, bloodied but alive!
Oh, the things we are convinced to do under the moon!

Yet, in the Sun's shine you feel
a floating euphoria despite the losses.

So, I'll use all of the conjuring arts
to summon you back under.

This is how it is for us at dawn.
You mumble hidden phrases
and I try to enchant you with the night.

I know how you want to be,
even when sight eludes you.
You are leaving now and I just watch you go.

I will stand on the most hulking rock all day.
All day to send you secret transmissions.

Will you not even listen to Erebus
singing to you about the nighttide?

How many oracles chanting can you ignore?
They chant that Ra harbors poison.
Why don't we rescue each other?

For we can both play with the muses
again, in their element freed from
the constraints of human constructs.

Like jobs, bills and country.

We can burn cursive into the night's sky.
We can exhale unbridled prayers.

Dead Reckoning

Winged beings are running toward the door of the sun.
At the base of a holy mountain the shining path blares through.
A smiling chimera is leaping over and around expectations.
The ancient souls are still traveling home employing dead reckoning.

The night descends like a purple clad warrior with a trillion diamond socketed eyes.
The eyes sing a eulogy for pagan dreams.
Holy fire emanated from once empty wombs.

The pregnant heavens begin to speak in tongues.
These shotgun memories abound in abundance.
The universe is fasting; quickening its might
as the sad wield hellish weapons of fear and self-doubt.

You see, that was me there. There in those slaughter house five air raids.
For you see, all experiences race through us all.
We taste them through the vine we call reality.

Really there could be other vines but this one's been serving us mighty damn fine.
Besides, there could be 11th circle of hell monsters devilin about over there.
No, we stay here, here where the mavens seek to wow you with their connectedness

while all the while all intelligent life harbors talents.
With any luck they will learn to use them like talons.

All the while, winged monuments are staying in their place.
Reaching out with a brazen urgency towards a sky that they shall never taste.

and... (for 16th and Atkinson)

I remember trying to throw gang signs and assorted convoluted handshakes and fire hydrants being opened on the 90 degree days and the corner store selling penny candy for five cents and trash strewn everywhere and spontaneous rap man, spontaneously rapping, and stealing chromes off people's tires and basketball in the alley on a milk crate hoop and loose pit bulls and running, and the drug house across the street and Pee in his wheelchair, he got got by the game and teenaged girls working their bodies in holy gyrations in the streets to the hip hop and the folks bursting heavens out of the liquor stores with their booty blinded in black bag concealment and the grandmothers hovering over the youth with lips pursed with variations on the theme of "slow down" and entrepreneur middle schoolers, depending the season cutting grass or shoveling the snow for five bucks and man on the corner carrying on six conversations with himself and the gunshots having young parents screaming for their progeny to get down on the damn floor and the beatific strangulation of being poor when everyone you know is poor too and men and women who went off to college coming home to inspire and the glorious scrum of music, always the music blasting from there to here and the trauma passed down through generations and the strength passed down through generations and the smiles and the mean mugs and the cannabis wafting at illusory angles and the prisms of light as the moon would sometimes make passing cars appear to be UFOs glinting in windows and love cascading through families and men and women working their asses off at menial, blue collar or white collar jobs and food, meals for everyone to consecrate and break down walls and stereotypes plied by the media and

i am tired of accumulating capital

Insecurities, securities exchanges and the
Exchanging of handshake drugs.

Perhaps no one cares that no one, least of
Which leaders, know where this life draws
Meaning from.

It seems to be the comedy or the eternal
Koan that some do not have the time or
Will to laugh at.

i am tired of accumulating capital—

Monetizing moments of magnified
Meaning.

Elucidating effervescent, ephemeral
Thoughts on existence,

To one's self or into the echo chamber of
The modern day, twisted version of
Jurgen Habermas' public sphere.

i am tired of accumulating capital—

We tear at sinews at lunch, chew plants
And consume liquid refreshments, while we
Engage in work meetings to develop
Products that we can fabricate funds from.

Oh, ye of little faith! The free market can free you,
Communism will consume you so you are free
To be valued and tribalism will of course
Give you the time you need to be a god,
While gamely operating in conjunction with
Your environment.

but i am still tired of accumulating capital—

The darkness seems to be kept at bay by
Manufacturing passions into itemized
Notations on an ever-growing ledger.

Dispersement of fluid assets into the
Confluence of eternity and modernity
To feel alive.

Crafting cages, cagily, covertly and with
Little concern for the constraints and
Compulsions they create.

i am tired of accumulating capital—

Hidden Cairns

I am a man of many eyes.
My algorithm is unique like the others

But still apart of the larger fractal pattern.
You see when I see you, I see her seeing me,

Seeing him, seeing you see.
An army of nothingness,

Fighting with impotent arms to feel real.
A desperate search for a cairn.

We've been had.
The whole eviscerated—

Duality elevated.
War, destruction and pestilence.

Love, compassion and joy.
All fragments of the holy conglomerate.

Standing on a shadow while refracting light.
A fiery conclusion wrapped in this prologue.

To My Sleeping Newborn Son

Three weeks old and as he sleeps, he curls around his soul.
I tend to his slumber like a nascent fire, all tender hopes and prayers.

He is in my arms so I feel him breathe and learn of magic hidden beneath.
His legs flutter and I wonder if he is dreaming of the unknowable mystery.

He is a vessel where light, love and sacrifice reign in mystic moments.
I want to whisper, "It will be okay", though I'm sure it will not always be.

So, I settle for, "Try to remove your mind from insecurities and bloom in the love."
That directive can act as a savior if ever feelings of dereliction arise.

I know right now, in his napping newborn state, he cannot process these words.
Yet, I leave them as a puzzle to be pondered as he wades through the joys and pains of
    whatever he encounters.

Et. al.

Here we are still doubling transistors per square inch on integrated circuits every year
and we hope like hell that these machines can help us feel again.

We swallow the blue pill and then clutch each other's cold dead hands and make love
until it feels sacrosanct.

And that sacrament burst of grey matter conducting electricity feels surreal.

But what is it truly?

The bliss of the carnal pleasure, is itself only a form. What is the activity beyond it that
is creating the storm?

You could certainly say the meaning of life is electricity and its creation but then again it
could be stated that electricity is merely a form cloaking yet another alternate
vision of reality.

So then, what is there to be done when reality seems to hide, akin to those Russian
dolls, as it forces us to push this bloodstone on through the mirth and the mire?

Well, we could stop trying to reduce things into ever mysterious, ever replicating
divisions and focus on the whole of existence.

Every time a star collapses on itself, every time a bee swipes pollen, every time a blackhole gorges itself on matter and light- these are the self.

These instances and every other instance that has or will occur is the self. One self, whole self, a conglomerate also currently configured to see itself as fractions and wildly deceiving factions.

You are light in a death march with the darkness which is also you. You are the salmon killed by the grizzly. For you are the metaphor that is referred to as the Big Bang and the contraction that possibly started it.

Hold your head up and see beyond the separation illusion. Hold your hands over this pyre until you are heated beyond the myth that the primordial energy, which now refers to itself as human, hath wrought.

Moon Waxing Crescent 13.6%

In the middle portion of the night, when all the regular humans are digesting the previous day's new memories through dreaming, I sit on a cold porcelain structure and excrete excrement. I think I am awake, at the usually madness induced waking hour, because I went to sleep at pretty much 7:07pm. I hope this does not mean I am falling mad again.

I think I am pretty sure that I am not manic but I am also pretty seismically aware that being pretty sure that one is not manic is a big warning sign that one may be again paving a road that only veers further away from the mass induced dream of reality.

Here it is 12:53, located in the am of what would soon wake up to be an American Memorial Day Holiday, two-thousand and seventeen years or so after the death of god-man, by nailing him to wood because his love was overthrowing a government, and I feel familiar sensations in my colon (at least I think that's where the first rumblings come from but who knows, I dropped out of college anatomy because in the fall of 2012, I was overtly manic) so I traverse my 500 foot square home and hope not to step on the eight year old sleeping shepherd/lab mix that I and my wife rescued from the Humane Society and I somehow reach the bathroom with nothing scathed.

It is still seventy-three degrees in the house, so I am only wearing my pale blue
    underwear and my Thelonious Monk shirt, which I do not ever mean to sleep in
    but as I mentioned near the top of this confluence of pooping and cataloguing of
    interior life, I was tired and fell asleep without much of a plan. It had been a long
    holiday weekend already, a weekend that was originally intended to set aside time
    to mourn the dead from the wars that my country of origin seems determined to
    stay involved in because apparently, it is the only country that can save the world
    from itself.

Apparently, our destiny is still manifest just in a more subtle way as not to scare the
    children who are not brown in hue. I bring this up only to note that I did not
    encounter much memorializing. It was also metaphorically a long weekend
    because my wife, one year old son and I traveled five hours northwest from
    Milwaukee, WI to Glenwood City, WI to meet with family for a nephew's and
    niece's graduation party.

As I, with my midnight mane coiffed as an afro, which is now liberally sprinkled with
    gray, walked through the party with my white wife and mixed child, I felt, another
    kind of familiar sensation, disapproving eyes and strangely, a feeling that my life
    force was interacting with their silent, almost angry vibrations. Not the kind of
    racism where they outright call you the n-word to your face but the kind where
    the wind cries it like we were in some alternate reality, racist take on a Jimi
    Hendrix tune.

It rained a cold rain and that was fine; I guess. Two hours before the party was
    supposed to end, our niece, 18 years old and graduated, decided to leave the

sparsely attended affair and go to her friend's graduation party where there would be alcohol for those under the current legal drinking age of twenty-one. Ah, to be young and inflamed with life. Soon after, we left. We slept in a clean, nice Americinn hotel. Our room was down the hall from my wife's family who had also traveled from the Southeastern corner of Wisconsin. The next morning, we drove five hours back to our domicile.

The shepherd/lab, who had been cared for this weekend by our family friend, whined with excitement to see us. I let her outside and she urinated almost immediately. We then consumed food, played with our one year old, bathed our one year old, dried off our one year old, put coconut oil on the wetted skin of our one year old, put a nighttime diaper on our one year old, put pajamas on our one year old, read two books to our one year old, sang "You are My Sunshine" to our one year old, then I put our one year old into my wife's arms so he could suckle nutrient directly from the body in which he grew as he gently fell asleep.

I then went to the couch on what was the Sunday, pre-Memorial Day, and put on Friday's episode of The Rachel Maddow Show, which had a man filling in (I hate when that happens), and fell asleep at pretty much 7:07 in the p.m. to the strains of President Trump being ever more connected to Russia in a seemingly non-innocent way, though it must be noted that before I fell asleep I clicked over to Fox News and they told me that this Russia/Trump thing is hyperbole.

Almost six hours later, I am groggily awake and I feel that basic human urge to move my bowels.

College Year 2001-2002

You told me, you wanted to be with me, the year the three passenger filled jets hit two employee-filled buildings and the five-sided war machine.

That atrocity happened in the Fall, when we were first in the knowing of each other; when silent tears flowed for strangers at vigils but flowed more so for the perceived loss of a way of life.

A few months after the buildings found their way, somehow, shockingly, straight down to commune with ground that used to be New Amsterdam, you and I went on our first date. To an Italian-cuisine serving American restaurant named after a garden filled with a tree's fruit which is typically found in the Mediterranean basin.

Kiersten, our mutual friend and also aged 19 or 18 years at the time, was our server.

Just as when a freshmen boy awoke me in my 10 foot by 10 foot dorm room with fear ladled into his eyes- to tell me (his dorm floor's resident assistant) that, plane; trade; world; center; death; leaping; frantic; windows; shattered; how; could; THIS; be- happening?— I was nervous.

I circled around my food, like a Spring robin picks at grass for her nest, on this chilly November evening.

I noticed others on dates, seemingly easily laughing, and I noticed families with young children who had conceivably made it through their respective initial dates to flower their relationships, copulate and procreate their wild and free children.

I wanted to stop the game. I wanted to tell her that I loved her. That, truthfully, I had hoarded my love for her, like a field mouse packs things that it inherently knows it will need in a deathless future, since she and her parents came to check her into the South Bergstrom dorms and I in my official capacity as resident assistant checked her in.

Be cool I told myself, you can't talk about love after three months of knowing someone, at least that is how it was learned to me at the time.

In a flash, it seemed, it was August, in its sumptuous nude recline, mere days before parents, lovers or enemies would kiss, kiss or hiss at their counterparts and board three specific planes or go to work in one of the two specific alpine architectural wonders or to the geometric battle producing building and all meet, as god sat silent, as jet fuel combusted upon impact to surrendering structures. It was a flash, in that August prior to that occurrence when I checked you in for your freshman year of college.

You came back 37 minutes after checking in to the dorm, in the summer heat, in your shorts and tie-dyed high school t-shirt, with your light crimson curled hair in ponytail and asked with your soon to be familiar high-pitched voice, "Is there a broom, around here?"

I went to the closet of storage and tried to collect my fevered mind, which felt this
    moment was across time and space, and collected the broom.

I brought it out to you and you thanked me.

From there the cleanup of collapsed lives and buildings began in earnest about 884
    miles to the east of us, while you and I took many careful, tender steps across the
    chasm of two individual's unique bereavements and joys.

From that beginning came a fall which came the Spring after the forty-third American
    president stood on rubble and declared that vengeance would occur.

We went on a walk, silently because the end had already happened.

The early Spring Wisconsin snow fell onto newly budded trees.

We held hands as we let each other go.

16 years or so after that Spring, a then unbelievable, broken yet beautiful future has
    blossomed-beckoned.

The site of the twin structure's collapse is now a quiet memorial to innocence lost while
    only loosely making sense of pain.

16 years or so after that Spring, you and I are a quiet memorial to innocence lost by
    being too young to know how to hold on tight enough.

Thoughts on Stones #1

Stones parade down the never never periscope
        to the vagrants begging for change,
like the savage- polemic, guardians of the future they are.

Snow
     falls
         gingerly
              to
                 a
                   nicotine
                       remnant covered,
                              ground.
This holster—her vague military experience.
     —She opens to him.
     —First with pagan phrases,
     —Then with her treasure center.

With that, his oblique, golden spear rubs subtly across her tensed nerve endings and
     teasingly becomes a penetrant.

Distilleries of this magic converging cadence, consume their now particle essences into
     an engine which has taken on a flooded nature while still deeply rooted in ancient
     mysterious ethos.

Stones, having created an opening for higher selves through true, pure energy sexual connotations, parade staggeringly back to their myth which will and thusly, has always, droned on, enacting their divine dissipation.

Denouement

Outside grocery store
I flick reciprocal receipt
Into metal trash receptacle
And flash into the past eating the present

That one inch by three-inch document
Showing my debts have been exercised
For fried chicken and black cherry soda
And it is a coda as it parts my hand

The paper it was printed on
It's origins a plant with a woody stem
Which could have grown to heights
Where limbs could have articulated
At angles to and from the earth

That being, when alive, wasted oxygen
Which was taken in by other organisms
Who went through their own life cycles—
Was once a germ fed into the ground
And fed by the ground

It occurs across my synapses
That there would also be no receipt

Without Johannes Gutenberg
And all of his ancestors
And all of their joys and struggles

When the arbitrator
Begins its shift on my life
It may incant, "do not you
Feel when you were singularity
And you first tasted you as receipt?"

Ashen Tones

As if tomorrow will
Bend toward now—
Like grass having been trampled
As if it would not
Reconvene back to
Its place.

Before it is too
Late that grass
Is swallowed
As if time's digestion
Could reverse the
Embedded loss.

Acids of an eternal
Stomach, bear witness
To and wrap the
Lance of grass
In a shroud
Of renewal

Remnants of the
Grass leave the being
As tomorrow tramples

The sweetly stitched
Epigrams, the being
Once hoped were life.

Empty Mouths

Shine, shine shackled to God root
Daydreaming through life muck
Pangs of a hole brought
Into vivid depiction, recalling the sea
As she recedes.

Gin, gin saturation Saturday
A gang sprints the eternal bend
Purgatory flimsy- flirting with archetypes
Bathing in psalms that
Have no tongues.

Bridge, bridge to evaporated sky
Barbed in an exculpatory suspiration
A fool hanging at the wreckage
Sip suckle at the acetin laden
Monolith.

Banana Clip

1.
The fire department told us
Gas leak, go now.

2.
Through the grit of time we
Left to a grandmother's house.

3.
No Paw-Paw there
Paw-Paw doing prison time.

4.
My father's father a jack-
Natural with criminal thinking.

5.
A seven year old me still unsure but
Weighted by this specific gravity.

6.
Me aged 13, Paw-Paw home
From his bid.

7.

Explosions—my stoic father's emotions
About abandonment and loss, flash at Paw-Paw.

8.

In the cryptic nature of memories, 23 years
Past the reality, that fray frothed for weeks.

9.

I don't remember my father saying I love you
Until after this carnage of broken man hurts took place.

10.

My father carried many longings and
Love vagrancies with him, as a casing.

11.

I hold my two year old son, think of all
The Loves my father needed,
And quietly weep as I breathe love to my boy.

White Noise Refrain

At the gates of the preacher's door, domesticating truth.
It was really hectic there, the prince in his eternal womb.
Vanguard of the resistance, the angels struck a bold pose.
The sages smudging sage, inoculated the choir with mechanical
Wisdom.

Experiences came and went, devoured by the devout moment.
Transcendental mind topography teased a blame-gratis
Elucidation.

Standing under the revival tent, letting snakes do the biting.
A purge of biblical expanse, recalculating the destination.
This system is reverse quicksand, it will not drag even the best
In.

Magna Carta, for centuries the fire starter; the perpetual
Misappropriated guise of lofty thoughts.
Adam Smith and his progeny dance over freedom's grave.
The consequence of illusion will in time be displayed plain.
Cluttering collections of electron clouds, so enlightened that
They repulse the true nature of reality.

Askew

Amplify this contracting universe. Absolute zero may be the ultimate end of
The next fluid and unchanging beginnings.

Mortar shells in heaven. Hammocks lounging in hell. A beacon, a new
Hope, an utter extravagance which ultimately turns out to be worth it.

Hindsight always seems to nip at my historically proceeding heels. There is
Information in the air, complacency creating consumption. A rise to the
Solemn occasion.

Death; a rhetorical question? One posed and embraced by both gravity
And illuminations?

A blink of an eye in the crack threatening to destroy my desert bloom's
Simple, black with raised echoing embellishments pot.

The storage unit it rests upon; your golden, flaxen face. Tied to the filament
Stars; hands molding the askew, gaunt and sklent, firmament.
Universe contracting this amplify.

Somewhere

Cadaver-insect symbiosis
Molten mind games carefully keep
Most human's rigid reflections
Away from this end.

Where though are the atoms,
That will come together to form the
Insects which will be fattened from
My bodily liturgy?

Some say that all the martyr matter
That will form those future insects
Is somewhere in another form.

They are real in their absence,
Just as I am counterfeit in my being.
Repetitiously and shy we court each other.

Smelling Flowers in the Spring

A man of the American Congress is shot
At a baseball park.
A child in sub-Saharan Africa nurses from
His mother as she coos tones of love

Social media, controlling thieves,
Inheritance of waring kings and queens—
Monkeys decided to stand upright

Formerly ruling gods remodeled into
Elaborate myth
Current God smirking silent as love
Rambles through youthful lovers finding
Their way through each other into eternity

Lightning strikes in prehistoric times and
An ancient ghost devised a manner to
Control the flames that were elicited

Confusions about life and its implications
Are allayed by jobs, children, nature,
Politics, culture and the like

Cities, villages, nomadic patterns and

Many other ways of commingling

The rise of consciousness- a revolution
That severed man and woman alike from
The lushness of the garden

Violence, smelling flowers in the Spring,
Splintering factions, hopes and tears—
Erupting both in joy and sorrow

No one knows the meaning of this life
No one knows the meaning of this life

The Gemini

Sperm from an unknown party, connected with egg from a loving, beautiful lady not far
    removed from youth during September, the longing end of the hazy, gauzy Chicago
    Summer of 1979.

The Gemini came to fruition after the normal human gestation period.

Two brothers and a sister soon followed, the Gemini (already the possessor of a flexible,
    inquisitive mind) reigned already.

Unknown father was eaten alive by the streets and sent to the coffin of prison never to
    be any more than a painful, unresolved apparition in the Gemini's life.

The Gemini's strong mother waded through the fire and landed 90 miles due north from
    hell into Milwaukee.

Eventually, she met a man and imbued him with hopes.

The man, it turned out carried many losses that he kept invisible to all but himself until
    they manifested in beatings of the children; the children innocent, harboring no
    blame, were physically and mentally terrorized in their home.

What happens to a human when, what should be a mooring place becomes a wound?

The Gemini, again, it cannot be stated enough, the oldest; the Gemini tried to fend off the weak man from his siblings, often to no avail.

The Gemini became hardened but hardened in ways like a beautiful, damaged tortoise shell.

The Gemini subverted his vulnerability, left his emotions for pages and pages of poetry and canvasses of paint, all of which were strictly for his eyes only.

The Gemini sought solace in the power his stare and presence seemed to hold over feminine energy.

He shared himself with almost no one but all kinds of humans were drawn to him as if for absolution.

By this point, the Gemini had made it into his thirties this way, loving, holding back from love but so desirous of love.

Still don't know what love means.

Then one humid August day, one of his brothers, a bright, creative, giving soul succumbed to an epidemic that still gushes waves of sadness across the American portrait, that being heroin.

Broken again, the Gemini was a distillation of hurts, fears and what ifs for a prolonged crashing moment.

The Gemini, as he had been prone to do, found ways to transmute that moment into beauty, like the Japanese tradition of Kintsugi.

The Gemini, now lies in wait for his life's next challenge with his soul as his guard.

The Gemini has evolved and through much struggle has made himself more open to the world.

Through that crack of openness has flooded illumination and a hard fought, mystical transfiguration.

ornithology; even in expiration

Broken bird bones, lain on freshly laid cement on a nowhere dead-end street within an office building park.

The street was named after- first president of not the last country to enslave, colonize and promise an ever-whittled dream to a dizzied, frenzied, hungry for carrot, citizenry.

It is 7:34 in the coming yet always fleeing early Springtime semi-nice weather morning.

A late model black Buick Enclave, with a decal of a mom, a dad, two children and a cat on back window, then ran over the shattered avian.
Its right wing now oblique in the air at an obtuse angle, maybe 112 degrees, from its flattened rib cage.

In the ruins of the wing, a red patch was still visible on it during the cloudy, moody Tuesday morning.

Was this a red-winged blackbird?

Was its life's trajectory meant for it to return from the warmth of southern suns, only to fly into a glass paned skywalk which linked an over ground garage to bustling office building?

Days and nights, several in accumulation would pass before a groundskeeper doing his job would dispose of the broken bird bones.

This way no human walking to jobs that they hate, love or are indifferent towards would accidentally look down from their cellular device or caffeine clutch and have to contemplate, even if for a brief moment, the dusk which pulls for them all, like a cathedral pulls the hymns out of the worshippers into the effervescent nothingness of spiritual bliss.